Build a Brand That Feels Like You

Neil J Milliner

Published by Neil Milliner, 2025.

BUILD A BRAND THAT FEELS LIKE YOU

First edition. September 12, 2025.

ISBN: 979-8232194406

Written by Neil J Milliner.

Contents

11. Next Steps & Validation

Boundary Scripts" for DMs, collabs, and interviews

Collection of Boundary Scripts for DMs, Collaborations, and Interviews
1. DM Boundaries
2. Collaboration Scripts
3. Interview & Public Appearance Scripts
4. Customization & Practice
Key Takeaways

"Visibility Audit" checklist

Visibility Audit Checklist
1. Channel Presence & Profile Alignment
2. Content Consistency & Cadence
3. Values & Messaging Alignment
4. Privacy & Boundary Compliance
5. Audience Engagement & Feedback
6. Technical Visibility Metrics
7. Accessibility & Inclusion
8. Action Planning & Review Cadence

Recap of "Build a Brand That Feels Like You"

This book equips privacy-conscious creators to anchor their brand in core values, set firm boundaries, and cultivate lasting impact—without burning out or oversharing.

1. Foundations: Values and Vision

2. Privacy and Boundaries

1. The Paradox of Public Privacy

Why visibility doesn't have to mean vulnerability

Redefining Visibility

VISIBILITY ISN'T A binary switch that flips you from hidden to exposed. It's a dial you control—one that lets you choose what to share, and when.

- Visibility as intentional signal, not open window
- How selective sharing builds credibility without overexposure
- Reframing fear of judgment into curiosity about your audience

The Safe Zones of Self-Disclosure

YOU CAN CONNECT DEEPLY without revealing every wound or worry. Safe zones are topics and formats where you feel ownership rather than regret.

- Process reveals: sharing how you work, not why you felt pain
- Idea snapshots: quick insights instead of full backstories
- Skill showcases: demonstrate competency without personal confession

Intentional Transparency Versus Overexposure

TRANSPARENCY BUILDS trust when it's aligned with your values. Overexposure breeds shame when you share before you're ready.

1. Define your threshold

- List three story topics that energize you

- List three story topics that drain you

1. Set time and format limits

- Live video for 5–10 minutes on wins and lessons
- Blog posts focused on strategy, not struggles

1. Review and adjust quarterly

- What resonated? What backfired?
- Fine-tune your disclosure dial

Case Studies of Quiet Visibility

ARTIST "M" USES A PSEUDONYM and voice-only podcast to discuss creative process. Coach "J" shares weekly strategy threads on Twitter without personal anecdotes.

CreatorVisibility TacticPrivacy Strategy
M
Voice-only podcast
No personal identifiers, no photos
J
Strategy threads
Threads focused on tactics, not trauma

Exercise: Mapping Your Comfort Spectrum

- Draw a horizontal line labeled "Private" on the left and "Public" on the right
- Plot topics you've shared (social media posts, stories) on that line
- Highlight three topics that always feel too far right—those are your "red zone"
- Develop one phrase you can use to redirect if someone

pushes you past that zone

Key Takeaways

- You control the dial of visibility—turn it up or down, as you choose
- Safe zones let you connect without sacrificing emotional safety
- Intentional transparency is a strategy; overexposure is often accidental
- Mapping your comfort clarifies where you'll thrive and where you'll retreat

Reframing "personal brand" as "intentional presence"

The Weight of "Personal Brand"

THE TERM PERSONAL BRAND often feels transactional and hollow. It suggests a one-size-fits-all marketing pitch rather than a genuine expression of who you are.

Introducing Intentional Presence

INTENTIONAL PRESENCE flips the script. It's less about crafting an image and more about choosing how, when, and why you show up. It foregrounds your values, your voice, and your boundaries over polished aesthetics.

- Centers on your core purpose rather than trending tactics
- Prioritizes meaningful connection over follower counts
- Embeds emotional safety—yours and your audience's—into every interaction

The Three Pillars of Intentional Presence

1. Core Values in Action

- Identify three non-negotiable principles that guide your work
- Use those values as the yardstick for every post, comment, or collaboration

1. Strategic Visibility

- Choose platforms and formats that align with your energy

levels
- Schedule high-engagement activities (like live Q&As) when you feel most prepared

1. Boundary-Built Connection

- Define what topics remain private, what's open for discussion, and why
- Script clear redirection phrases to maintain comfort zones

Exercise: Craft Your Intentional Presence Statement

1. List your top three professional values (for example: empathy, curiosity, creativity).
2. Describe the primary impact you want to make on your audience (for example: inspire confidence in timid learners).
3. Name one boundary you'll enforce to protect your wellbeing (for example: no DMs after 7 PM).
4. Combine these into a single sentence:

- "I show up with [value 1], [value 2], and [value 3] to [impact statement], while [boundary statement]."

Key Takeaways

- Intentional presence shifts focus from image-making to values-led engagement.
- Three pillars—values, visibility strategy, and boundaries—anchor your authentic voice.
- A concise presence statement ensures every public move aligns with who you truly are.

Case studies: Quiet creators who thrive

Case Studies: Quiet Creators Who Thrive

BELOW ARE THREE CREATORS who turned understated visibility into sustainable influence—without sacrificing privacy or emotional safety.

CreatorPlatform & TacticKey StrategiesResults
Niharikaa Kaur Sodhi
LinkedIn & Medium writing

- Consistent, process-focused articles
• Documents tactics, not trauma
• Sells cohort-based courses
- 89K+ LinkedIn followers
• Quit her 9–5 to create full-time

EcoCraftElle
Instagram micro-niche account

- Unedited DIY sustainable-living tutorials
• Active DM Q&As
• Highlights community creations
- ~8K followers
• 10% average engagement rate
• Collaborations with eco-brands

"M" (Pseudonymous Podcaster)
Voice-only weekly podcast

- Uses a pseudonym
• Focuses on creative-process interviews
• No personal identifiers or images
- 5K subscribers
• 15% listener-to-patron conversion

Spotlight on Strategies

- Niharikaa positions herself as a guide by sharing granular "how" over "why," building authority without oversharing her personal life.
- EcoCraftElle leverages authenticity: raw visuals and one-on-one replies become her signature, driving deep trust in a focused niche.
- M's audio-only format creates intimacy without visual or personal overexposure, inviting listeners into creative conversations—never into private life.

THESE CASE STUDIES demonstrate that strategic restraint and community-first content can outshine volume and vulnerability every time.

2. Your Essence Is Enough

Exercises to uncover your core values, tone, and energy

Exercise: Unearth Your Core Values

START BY MINING THE moments in your life that felt most alive. These flashes of energy point directly to what you value most.

1. Reflect on three turning points

- Describe each moment in one sentence (e.g., "When I taught my first student, I felt unstoppable").
- Next to each, note what quality was honored (e.g., creativity, empowerment, clarity).

1. Spot the common threads

- Look across your three moments. Which qualities repeat?
- Circle the top three that light you up every time you think of them.

1. Validate with contrast

- List two situations that left you drained or resentful.
- For each, write which of your chosen values was contradicted.

1. Finalize your core values

- Refine your list to three statements, each framed as "I honor ____ by ____."
- Example: "I honor curiosity by asking questions before sharing answers."

Exercise: Discover Your Authentic Tone

YOUR TONE IS THE EMOTIONAL filter you pour through every email, post, and caption. Let's pin it down.

1. Gather three samples

- Pick three pieces of writing or speech you love (could be TED talks, blog posts, song lyrics).
- Note what feels magnetic about each: is it playful? Fierce? Reassuring?

1. Extract mood words

- From each sample, pull out five adjectives that describe its personality.
- You'll end up with a list of 15–20 mood words.

1. Cluster & choose

- Group similar adjectives (e.g., warm, cozy, nurturing).
- Select your top three clusters—those will become "Your Tone Trio."

1. Test your trio

- Write a 50-word bio or tagline using only your Tone Trio and one core value.
- Read it aloud: does it feel unmistakably "you"? Revise until it does.

Exercise: Map Your Energy Rhythms

KNOWING WHEN YOU'RE at your best lets you plan visibility around your natural flow.

1. Daily energy log

- Over five days, record energy levels every two hours (High / Medium / Low).
- Note what you were doing and how you felt.

1. Plot your peaks and pits

- Draw a horizontal timeline (6 AM–10 PM) on a sheet.
- Mark your High, Medium, Low slots in three colors.

1. Align tasks to energy

- Assign creative, public–facing tasks to your High zones.
- Reserve Medium zones for batch work (scheduling, edits).
- Use Low zones for rest, research, or unstructured play.

1. Draft your "Energy Schedule"

- Create a weekly template that slots social posts, live sessions, and writing sprints into the right buckets.
- Circle one "experiment day" each week to tweak timing and format.

Key Takeaways

- Your three core values become the North Star for every brand decision.
- A Tone Trio—three mood clusters—ensures every word rings true.
- Energy mapping turns guesswork into a rhythm you can rely on.

How to build resonance without oversharing

How to Build Resonance Without Oversharing

RESONANCE COMES FROM speaking to shared human truths rather than broadcasting private details. When you focus on universal insights, readers lean in—even without intimate confessions.

Center on Universal Themes

CHOOSE TOPICS THAT tap into common emotions and experiences.

- Fear of failure, curiosity, longing for belonging, creative block
- Frame each piece around the lesson, not the personal backstory
- Use broad descriptions ("I hit a wall in my project") instead of specific triggers

Show Process, Skip the Trauma

LET YOUR AUDIENCE IN on how you work without unpacking every wound.

1. Break down a challenge into clear steps
2. Highlight the decision points and mindsets that moved you forward
3. Close with the insight you gained, not the pain you felt

Invite Reflection Through Questions

ENGAGE READERS BY HANDING them the pen.

- "What small choice could shift your week?"
- "When was the last time you turned uncertainty into action?"
- End posts or captions with a single open-ended prompt

Use Metaphors and Analogies

ABSTRACT IMAGES LET readers project their own stories.

- Compare creative flow to a river's current
- Describe boundary-setting as building a garden fence
- Keep metaphors tight—one per post or paragraph

Leverage Data and Stories in Tandem

NUMBERS LEND AUTHORITY; anecdotes spark connection—without oversharing.

- Lead with a statistic ("85 percent of creatives hit burnout within their first year")
- Follow up with a one- or two-sentence scenario that illustrates the data
- Skip names, dates, or identifying details

Exercise: Convert a Confessional into a Connector

1. Choose a snippet where you've shared deep emotion or detail.
2. Strip out specifics (names, dates, personal triggers).
3. Identify the core insight or lesson you want to convey.
4. Rewrite as:

- One-sentence setup ("I used to dread brainstorming sessions.")

- Three bullet points of what you did differently
- A closing question inviting readers to share their own tactics

Key Takeaways

- Resonance hinges on relevance and relatability, not raw vulnerability.
- Process-focused storytelling lets you teach without trauma.
- Strategic questions and metaphors create space for readers to connect.

Emotional safety in storytelling

Emotional Safety in Storytelling

STORYTELLING INVITES connection, but sharing too much can reopen old wounds or unsettle readers. Creating emotional safety means choosing what to reveal, how to frame it, and when to pause. It's a practice of self-respect as much as audience care.

- Define your emotional boundaries: know which topics energize you and which trigger discomfort
- Use content warnings or framing sentences to prepare readers for sensitive topics
- Emphasize insight over intimacy, so the story teaches rather than retraumatizes

Maintaining safety starts before you write. Check in with yourself: are you ready to revisit this memory? If the answer is no, postpone or rethink the angle.

1. Pause for a self-check: rate your readiness to tell this story from 1 (avoid entirely) to 5 (share freely)
2. Identify safety anchors: phrases or rituals you use to ground yourself (for example, deep breaths or a short break)
3. Draft with distance: write in third-person or use metaphor to create a buffer between you and the memory

Exercise: Crafting a Safe Story Blueprint

- Choose a lesson you want to share without diving into trauma
- Outline the context in three bullet points, focusing on

environment and actions, not emotions

- State the insight or transformation in one sentence
- Add one sentence framing for your audience ("This story taught me that..." or "Here's what I discovered when...")

Key Takeaways

- Emotional safety protects both storyteller and audience from unnecessary harm
- Boundaries, warnings, and framing create a container for sharing
- A safe story blueprint keeps focus on lessons rather than wounds

3. Boundaries Are Branding

How to set limits that protect your peace and still connect

How to Set Limits That Protect Your Peace and Still Connect

MAINTAINING BOUNDARIES doesn't mean ghosting your audience—it means choosing when, where, and how you engage so you can show up fully present without burning out.

Define Your Non-Negotiables

LIST THE CONDITIONS under which you will not compromise your well-being.

- Identify three engagement scenarios that energize you (e.g., 1:1 coaching calls, scheduled Q&As).
- Identify three scenarios that drain you (e.g., late-night DMs, unscheduled meetups).
- Frame each as a "yes" zone or "no" zone and revisit quarterly.

Craft Clear Communication Scripts

PREPARE BRIEF, RESPECTFUL phrases that reinforce your boundaries without confusion.

1. When you need to pause DMs:

- "I'm off-screen after 7 PM, but I'll reply first thing tomorrow."

1. When a collaboration request misses your brief:

- "Thanks for reaching out! I only take guest posts on topics aligned with my core values—here's my topic guide."

1. When you need to reschedule:

- "I'm grateful for your interest. My next open slot is two weeks away—does that work for you?"

Time-Box Your Engagement

ALLOCATE SPECIFIC WINDOWS for public interaction to avoid constant availability.

- Block "Community Hours" on your calendar (e.g., Tue/Thu 1–2 PM for comments and replies).
- Turn off notifications outside those windows.
- Use an away message to redirect real-time questions to scheduled sessions.

Signal Your Availability

MAKE YOUR BOUNDARIES visible so your audience knows what to expect.

- Add an "Office Hours" section to your bio or website.
- Post a weekly update: "This Friday I'll be live from 10–11 AM EST—drop your questions below!"
- Use status indicators on chat platforms (e.g., "Do Not Disturb" vs. "Open for Chats").

Exercise: Create Your Boundary Blueprint

1. Draw two columns—"Connection" and "Containment."
2. Under Connection, list three formats you love (e.g., live

video, email newsletter, voice notes).

3. Under Containment, list three limits you'll enforce (e.g., no unscheduled calls, 24-hour DM response time).
4. Write one paragraph that you'll share publicly, explaining your "why" and your new blueprint.

Key Takeaways

- Boundaries become part of your brand story when they're communicated with clarity and kindness.
- Scripts and signals turn abstract limits into practical touchpoints.
- Time-boxing transforms random overwhelm into predictable, sustainable connection.

Scripts and reframes for "selective transparency"

Scripts and Reframes for "Selective Transparency"

SELECTIVE TRANSPARENCY means sharing with intention—enough to connect, but never so much that you lose control. Below are six ready-to-use scripts plus reframes to keep your story focused, safe, and strategic.

1. The Process-Only Disclosure

SCRIPT: "I spent weeks experimenting with three different workflows before landing on the one that finally clicked. Here's how I broke down each step..."

Reframe Tip: Swap out personal pain points for clear milestones. Focus on the "what" and "how," not the "why it hurt."

2. The Lesson-Pivot Preface

SCRIPT: "After a handful of false starts, I realized that consistency beats perfection. That insight changed everything for me—here's what I tried next."

Reframe Tip: Lead with the insight you want readers to carry forward, then backfill with just enough context to make it credible.

3. The "Partial Peek" Teaser

SCRIPT: "I won't dive into every late-night email that made me question my path, but here's the one message that changed my mindset overnight."

Reframe Tip: Acknowledge depth without unpacking it. Promise deeper stories on your own terms—perhaps in a paid workshop or private newsletter.

4. The Boundary-Laying Preface

SCRIPT: "I love sharing strategy and wins, but I keep my family life out of the spotlight. Today, I'm walking you through the exact tactic that doubled my email open rates."

Reframe Tip: State your "no-go" zones upfront, then immediately deliver value on a topic you do want to explore.

5. The Redirect-and-Invite

SCRIPT: "That's a bit outside my usual lane, but I can share how I approached client pitches—which might help you, too. Here's a simple framework to try."

Reframe Tip: When asked a question you don't want to answer, thank them, then steer back to your expertise or preferred topic.

6. The Elevated Anecdote

SCRIPT: "In one pivotal meeting, I discovered that asking two simple questions unlocks collaboration every time. Here's the story—and the questions."

Reframe Tip: Tell just enough of the moment to illustrate the breakthrough. Skip the emotional setup and zero in on the "aha" takeaway.

Key Takeaways

- Always lead with value: your audience remembers insights, not overshares.
- A brief boundary statement empowers you to steer conversations.

- Reframes let you acknowledge depth without losing emotional safety.

Designing your "no-go zones" with confidence

Designing Your "No-Go Zones" with Confidence

NO-GO ZONES ARE NON-negotiable boundaries that safeguard your emotional and creative wellbeing. Designing them with confidence means knowing exactly what you will not share, why it matters, and how to communicate it—so you can show up fully present in the areas you choose.

Why No-Go Zones Matter

YOUR AUDIENCE RESPECTS clarity. When you define what's off-limits, you:

- Protect your privacy and mental energy
- Build trust by being transparent about your limits
- Focus attention on the topics where you genuinely want to engage

Spotting Your Personal Red Lines

IDENTIFY THEMES OR scenarios that consistently drain or unsettle you:

1. Recall three moments when you felt exposed or drained after sharing.
2. List the topics or questions that triggered that discomfort.
3. Notice patterns: are they about relationships, finances, health, or something else?
4. Group similar items into distinct "no-go" categories.

Framing and Naming Your No-Go Zones

A CLEAR NAME ANCHORS each boundary in your mind and your audience's:

- Relationship Radar: topics about family or intimate life
- Money Map: any talk of personal income, pricing, or financial hardship
- Health Horizon: details about physical or mental health struggles

Attach a simple rationale: "I keep my family out of my brand to preserve their privacy" or "I don't share my earnings to keep the focus on strategy, not numbers."

Sharing Your Limits with Clarity

TURN ABSTRACT BOUNDARIES into concrete signals for your community:

No-Go ZoneDescriptionHow to Communicate

Relationship Radar

No details on family or romantic life

"I'm here to talk strategy—my personal world stays offline."

Money Map

No discussion of personal finances

"I share pricing guidelines, but personal earnings are private."

Health Horizon

No deep dives on health challenges

"I focus on creative methods—health journeys stay personal."

Exercise: Your No-Go Zone Blueprint

1. Create three columns labeled "Zone," "Why," and "Script."
2. In "Zone," write each no-go category you identified.
3. In "Why," jot a brief rationale for the boundary.
4. In "Script," craft a one-sentence phrase you'll use to redirect conversations.
5. Review quarterly and refine based on new insights or comfort shifts.

Key Takeaways

- No-go zones are your brand's silent guardians: define them to stay true.
- Naming and framing each boundary gives you and your audience a clear map.
- A simple script transforms your limits into confident, value-driven signals.
- Regular check-ins ensure your no-go zones evolve with your growth.

4. The Persona Spectrum

From pseudonyms to alter-egos: choosing your public-facing self

4.1 From Pseudonyms to Alter-Egos: Choosing Your Public-Facing Self

FINDING THE RIGHT MASK lets you show up with confidence, control what people see, and guard what remains private. Your public persona can be as close to your everyday self or as dramatically different as an alter-ego—but it should always feel true to your values and energy.

4.1.1 The Persona Spectrum

THINK OF YOUR PUBLIC identity as a slider with four main positions:

1. Real Name

- Full transparency, highest authenticity
- Least privacy: every post ties directly back to you

1. Nickname or Initials

- Slight distance, still recognizable
- Good for creators who want a hint of separation

1. Pseudonym

- A crafted name unlinked from your personal identity
- Common for writers, podcasters, or visual artists

1. Full Alter-Ego

- A distinct character with its own voice, style, and story
- Maximum creative freedom and privacy shield

4.1.2 Choosing Your Zone on the Slider

USE THESE CRITERIA to land on the right spot:

- Alignment with Values • Does this name or character reflect your core principles? • Will it honor your boundaries long-term?
- Privacy Needs • How much of your real life do you want off-limits? • Will this persona allow you to retreat when you need to?
- Clarity and Recall • Is it easy to spell, remember, and pronounce? • Does it stand out in your industry or niche?
- Creative Fit • Does an alter-ego open up storytelling possibilities? • Or does a simpler pseudonym feel more genuine for your message?

4.1.3 Spotlight Examples

- Banksy (Pseudonym): A single name that shrouds identity and fuels creative mystique.
- J.K. Rowling → Robert Galbraith (Pseudonym): Shifted genres without fanfare or preconceptions.
- Marshall Mathers → Eminem (Alter-Ego): Amplified a performance persona distinct from his private life.

EACH CHOSE A DIFFERENT point on the spectrum to protect themselves, serve their art, and connect with audiences on their own terms.

4.1.4 Exercise: Map Your Persona Options

1. List four name ideas—ranging from your real name to a bold alter-ego moniker.
2. Beside each, note the level of privacy it offers (High, Medium, Low).
3. Sketch a brief description of the voice or character traits you'd adopt.
4. Share these with a trusted colleague or friend and get feedback on which feels most "you."

4.1.5 Key Takeaways

- Your public-facing self is a tool: choose the level of separation that fits your comfort and goals.
- A pseudonym can be enough to create safe distance; an alter-ego invites playful reinvention.
-

Visual identity that reflects without exposing

4.2 Visual Identity That Reflects Without Exposing

YOUR VISUAL IDENTITY is the silent ambassador of your brand—subtle yet powerful, it conveys mood and values without revealing personal details. By choosing colors, shapes, and imagery that echo your essence, you draw in the right audience while keeping private the things that matter most.

4.2.1 Why Visual Identity Matters

A COHESIVE VISUAL IDENTITY

- Signals professionalism and consistency
- Reinforces your core values without a single word
- Shields personal aspects by focusing on symbolism over self-portraiture

Crafting visuals that resonate begins with understanding that your brand's look isn't a selfie—it's a mirror of your principles and style.

4.2.2 Elements of Privacy-Conscious Branding

ELEMENTPURPOSEPRIVACY-Friendly Approach

Color Palette

Evokes mood (warmth, calm, energy)

Select abstract palettes (sunset gradients, nature tones)

Typography

Conveys tone (playful, formal, modern)

Use custom fonts or type treatments instead of hand-written

Logo & Symbols
Anchors recognition
Design geometric or abstract icons that hint at your niche
Photography Style
Humanizes brand
Opt for silhouettes, object shots, or masked/anonymous models
Patterns & Textures
Adds depth and uniqueness
Create repeats from meaningful shapes (e.g., waves for flow)

4.2.3 Designing with Intention

1. Define your emotional keywords

- Choose three mood words (e.g., serene, bold, playful) from your Tone Trio.

1. Build a mood board

- Collect color swatches, font samples, and abstract images that align with those words.

1. Abstract your story

- Translate personal symbols (a bridge you cross, a mountain you climb) into simple iconography.

1. Test at scale

- Mock up your logo and palette on social posts, headers, and business cards to ensure readability and resonance.

4.2.4 Exercise: Your Privacy-First Brand Kit

1. Create a new folder named "Brand Kit" on your device.
2. Inside, add three subfolders: Colors, Fonts, Imagery.
3. Colors

- Pin five swatches that feel aligned but not tied to any personal photo.

1. Fonts

- Choose two primary fonts and one accent typeface that speak your tone.

1. Imagery

- Gather three visuals: one abstract shape, one silhouette or object shot, one pattern.

1. Assemble a one-page PDF or slide showing how these elements work together.

4.2.5 Key Takeaways

- Focus on symbolic visuals that echo your values, not your face or personal life.
- A well-chosen palette and typography speak volumes about your tone and energy.
- Abstract icons and silhouettes humanize without overexposure.
- A simple brand kit keeps your visual identity consistent and privacy-proof.

How to be magnetic without being manic

4.3 How to Be Magnetic Without Being Manic

CULTIVATING MAGNETIC presence means drawing people in with calm confidence, not frantic frequency. It's about creating moments of genuine connection that leave space for your audience to breathe—and come back for more.

4.3.1 The Magnetic Mindset

EVERY MAGNETIC MOMENT starts with intent.

- Prioritize resonance over reach: aim to touch hearts, not just eyeballs
- Embrace steady cadence rather than content chaos
- Honor your energy limits—consistency breeds trust, burnout erodes it
- Build curiosity by showing just enough, then inviting questions

4.3.2 Principles of Balanced Visibility

1. Space to Breathe

- Alternate between spotlight posts and quieter value drops
- Let ideas sit so your audience can marinate on them

1. Quality Over Quantity

- Invest time in one thoughtful insight instead of three rushed ones
- Leverage your Tone Trio to ensure every message feels

unmistakably "you"

1. Rhythm, Not Rush

- Establish a predictable schedule (e.g., weekly deep dive, biweekly Q&A)
- Use templates and workflows to streamline creation without sacrificing heart

1. Invitation, Not Interruption

- End posts with open-ended prompts rather than demands
- Frame CTAs as genuine offers to help, not pressure to buy

4.3.3 Strategies to Captivate Calmly

1. Tease and Deliver

- Start with a concise hook that poses a question or promise
- Follow up within the same post (or next touchpoint) with clear insight

1. Build in Pauses

- Break copy into short lines or use bullet lists for skimmability
- In videos, pause between ideas—let silence reinforce the point

1. Anchor in Values

- Weave your three core values into examples and metaphors
- Repetition of values signals authenticity and cohesion

1. Invite Co-Creation

- Ask your audience to share their own experiences or tips
- Highlight a reader's response in your next post to deepen engagement

1. Reflect Before Responding

- Batch your engagement to set boundaries (see 3.3.3)
- Take a moment to craft a thoughtful reply rather than answering on impulse

4.3.4 Exercise: Draft Your Magnetic Yet Measured Hook

1. Choose a single insight you want to share (e.g., "Why less planning can spark more creativity").
2. Write a 20-word hook that teases the benefit without oversharing your backstory.
3. Expand in three bullet points:

- What the insight is
- How to apply it
- An invitation to share one's own experience

1. Review for tone and pacing: remove any jargon or excess flair that distracts.
2. Test it on a friend or in a small group—note their reaction and adjust for clarity and calm impact.

4.3.5 Key Takeaways

- Magnetism arises from intentional restraint, not relentless output.
- Space, rhythm, and invitation turn passive scrollers into

active participants.

- A well-crafted hook and paced delivery keep your presence compelling without chaos.
- Grounding every piece in your core values ensures authenticity shines through.

5. Content That Connects Without Confession

Formats that foster trust without trauma

Formats That Foster Trust Without Trauma

PRESENTING CONTENT in structured, value-first formats lets you build credibility without revisiting personal wounds. Below are seven formats—each designed to deliver insight, spark engagement, and honor emotional safety.

Key Formats Overview

FORMATDESCRIPTIONWHY It Builds TrustPrivacy Level

Tip-Driven Lists

Concise lists of actionable steps (e.g., "5 Ways to...").

Readers absorb clear advice and feel immediate benefit.

Very High

Micro-Case Studies

Short, anonymized success stories with outcome and lessons.

Demonstrates real-world impact without personal disclosure.

High

Data-Backed Insights

Combine relevant statistics with brief commentary or recommendations.

Lends authority and detaches from personal narrative.

Very High

Question-First Prompts

Open-ended questions paired with a framework for response.

Invites reader reflection and positions you as facilitator.

Very High

Expert Roundups

Collate top tips from peers or industry voices on a given topic.

Leverages collective credibility, keeping your story in the background.

High

Hypothetical Scenarios

"Imagine you..." situations that walk readers through choices.

Creates empathy and learning through projection, not confession.

High

Resource Curation

Lists of tools, books, or articles annotated with your takeaways.

Shows you've done the research and directs readers to safe, reputable sources.

Very High

Best Practices for Safe, Trustworthy Content

- Lead with value: start every piece by stating the benefit or takeaway.
- Keep personal context minimal: use "we" or "people" instead of "I" when possible.
- Use neutral language: replace emotionally loaded words (e.g., "traumatized") with objective terms (e.g., "challenges," "roadblocks").
- Frame calls to action as invitations: "Feel free to share" rather than "Let me know if you're struggling."
- Offer optional deeper dives: link to gated worksheets or private newsletters for readers seeking more detail.
- Provide content warnings when touching on sensitive topics, and always pair with a strengths-oriented reframing.

Sample Format Blueprint: Tip-Driven List

1. Title: "5 Quick Ways to Overcome Creative Block"
2. Intro paragraph (2–3 sentences): state the common challenge

and promise solutions.

3. Numbered list of tips (50–75 words each):

- Action step
- Brief "why it works"

1. Closing question: "Which tip will you try today?"
2. Optional resource link: "Download our worksheet for deeper practice."

Exercise: Choose Your Signature Format

1. Review the table above and pick two formats that align with your energy rhythms.
2. Sketch a raw outline for each, focusing on:

- Core topic or question
- Three to five key points or examples
- A clear invitation for reader reflection or next steps

1. Share your outlines with a peer group for feedback on clarity and tone.

Key Takeaways

- Structured, value-first formats build authority without unnecessary vulnerability.
- Tables, lists, data, and hypothetical scenarios offer trust without trauma.
- Framing language and content warnings preserve emotional safety.
- Selecting one or two signature formats simplifies your content process and amplifies consistency.

How to share your process, not your pain

How to Share Your Process, Not Your Pain

DIRECT ANSWER: CENTER every story on actions, tools, and outcomes—strip out the trauma, spotlight your method, and invite readers to learn and apply.

Why Process-First Storytelling Wins

SHARING PROCESS OVER pain...

- Builds trust through expertise rather than sympathy
- Keeps emotional safety intact for you and your audience
- Positions you as a guide who illuminates paths, not wounds

Five Steps to Reveal Method, Not Meltdown

1. Identify Your Key Phases

BREAK YOUR WORK INTO 3–5 clear stages (for example: research, prototyping, testing, refinement).

- Name each phase in a way that hints at progress ("Ideation Spark," "Blueprint Draft").
- Note one tool or approach you use at each stage.

2. Detail Tools and Techniques

PEOPLE WANT ACTIONABLE insights.

- List software, prompts, or questions you ask yourself.
- Share short "how-to" bullets—no more than one sentence

each.

3. Use Neutral, Object-Focused Language

SWAP OUT EMOTIONAL adjectives for concrete descriptors.

- Instead of "I felt crushed by rejection," write "I received three rounds of edits."
- Describe what happened, not how you felt.

4. Highlight Outcome and Insight

EVERY PROCESS SHARE needs a payoff.

- Quantify the result ("Cut my draft time by 40%") or describe the breakthrough ("Discovered a template that renewed my momentum").
- End with a one-sentence takeaway—your distilled lesson.

5. Invite Reader Application

TURN PASSIVE READERS into active experimenters.

- Ask a direct question ("Which step will you try first?").
- Offer a mini-challenge ("Map your own four-phase process and share one phase below").

Before & After: From Pain to Process

CONFESSIONAL POST (Pain-First)Process-First Rewrite

"I spent weeks sobbing over my failed launch and doubting myself."

"After three rounds of feedback, I pivoted my launch strategy. Here's the checklist I followed in each review cycle."

Too much emotion, not enough action
Focused on steps, tools, and repeatable framework

Exercise: Process-Only Rewrite

1. Choose a draft where you share a struggle.
2. Underline every feeling word (doubt, fear, overwhelm).
3. Replace each underlined phrase with:

- A stage name ("Iteration Two")
- A tool or question you used ("I asked, 'What if I reverse this order?'")

1. Add a closing outcome sentence and one reader prompt.

Key Takeaways

- Process stories teach; pain stories entertain at the cost of safety.
- Neutral language and clear phases transform vulnerability into value.
- Inviting readers to act cements your role as mentor, not therapist.

Building audience intimacy through insight, not access

Building Audience Intimacy Through Insight, Not Access

DIRECT ANSWER: DEEPEN connection by sharing contextualized takeaways, thought processes, and curated frameworks—so your readers feel seen and guided without needing backstage passes to your private life.

Why Insight Trumps Access

YOUR AUDIENCE CRAVES relevance and resonance more than a peek behind the curtain.

- Insight feels purposeful; access can feel voyeuristic
- Teaching frameworks invites co-creation; personal gossip isolates
- Guiding questions spark reflection; unfiltered confessions risk overwhelm

Four Techniques to Forge Intimate Bonds

1. Contextualized Case Examples

- Share anonymized scenarios drawn from your work or your readers' journeys
- Highlight decision points, pivot moments, and subtle mindset shifts

1. Personalized Hypotheticals

- Invite readers to place themselves in a situation: "Imagine you..."
- Walk them through choices and likely outcomes, then ask for their take

1. "Peek My Notebook" Insights

- Post snapshots of your annotated frameworks or mind-map snippets
- Use redacted labels or blurred sections to preserve private details

1. Reflective Prompts and Micro-Surveys

- End each post with one focused question or poll ("Which step felt hardest?")
- Collect feedback and share aggregated themes (not individual responses)

Example Insight-First Post Blueprint

SECTIONWHAT TO INCLUDE

Hook

A relatable challenge ("Stuck drafting your intro?")

Context

A brief, anonymized setup ("A client hit this wall last week.")

Insight

The core lesson or framework ("Try this three-step outline.")

Visual Aid

Diagram, template excerpt, or blurred screenshot

Invitation

One sharp question or micro-prompt

Exercise: Craft Your First Insight Touchpoint

1. Identify a recurring question or roadblock in your audience.
2. Write a two-sentence anonymized scenario that captures it.
3. Distill your go-to solution into three clear bullet points.
4. Choose one visual or prompt to reinforce the framework.
5. End with a single open-ended question to invite sharing.

Key Takeaways

- Intimacy born from insight feels empowering, not invasive.
- Framing content as guided discovery positions you as mentor, not performer.
- Strategic prompts turn passive readers into engaged collaborators.
- A clear post blueprint ensures every piece deepens trust without oversharing.

6. Visibility Without Burnout

Sustainable strategies for showing up

Sustainable Strategies for Showing Up

DIRECT ANSWER: DESIGN energy-aligned rhythms, batch and template your work, set firm boundaries, and embed recovery rituals so that showing up becomes a renewing practice, not a draining obligation.

Why Sustainable Presence Matters

CREATING CONSISTENCY without burnout preserves your creative spark and builds audience trust.

When you show up from a place of rest and focus, every piece of content feels intentional, not forced.

Core Pillars of a Sustainable Presence

- energy management
- boundary setting
- content scaffolding
- recovery practice

EACH PILLAR SUPPORTS your ability to deliver value without depleting yourself.

Four Techniques to Keep You Showing Up

1. Thematic Batching

- Group related topics into one production session
- Repurpose the batch across blog posts, newsletters, and social snippets

1. Modular Templates

- Create fill-in-the-blank outlines for stories, case studies, or micro-lessons
- Swap in new examples without reinventing structure

1. Energy Windows

- Map your peak creative hours and reserve them for high-value tasks
- Slot administrative or low-cognition tasks into off-peak windows

1. Accountability Loops

- Partner with a peer for weekly check-ins on your deliverables
- Share progress publicly in a small group for built-in momentum

Example Weekly Rhythm

DAYMORNING FOCUSAFTERNOON FocusRecovery Ritual

Monday

Brainstorm next week's themes

Draft two modular outlines

15-minute mindful walk

Tuesday

Record audio or video batch

Quick edits and uploads

Sketch or free-write session

Wednesday

Admin (emails, comments)

Guest collaboration calls

30-minute yoga stretch

Thursday
Deep work on flagship content
Start repurposing snippets
Short guided meditation
Friday
Final edits and scheduling
Audience feedback review
Social-media-free afternoon
Weekend
Light check-ins (optional)
Inspiration gathering
Nature outing or digital detox

Exercise: Design Your Sustainable Rhythm

1. Track your energy levels hourly for three days.
2. Identify your two peak creative windows.
3. Choose one day for batching and one day for recovery.
4. Outline three modular templates you can reuse.
5. Share your draft rhythm with an accountability partner for feedback.

Key Takeaways

- Align tasks with natural energy cycles to maintain flow.
- Batching and templates multiply your output without extra strain.
- Clear boundaries protect both your creativity and well-being.
- Recovery rituals refill your tank and spark fresh insights.

NEXT WE CAN EXPLORE automations and tools to streamline your batches, or dive into guest features and collaborations to spread the workload. Which direction feels most exciting right now?

Social media with soul (and boundaries)

Social Media with Soul (and Boundaries

DIRECT ANSWER: INFUSE each post with your core values and a clear "off-limits" framework—so you spark genuine connection without sacrificing your energy, privacy, or creative center.

Why Soulful Social Media Matters

SHOWING UP WITH PURPOSE transforms scrolling into meaningful exchange.

Soulful posts build trust faster than polished broadcasts, and they invite readers into a two-way conversation rather than a one-sided monologue.

Boundaries protect your wellbeing, ensuring your social channels remain a source of inspiration instead of exhaustion.

Four Core Principles

- Values-First Content Anchor every update in one of your guiding values—clarity, compassion, curiosity, or creativity.
- Intentional Frequency Publish with a sustainable cadence, then lean back and give yourself room to recharge.
- Reciprocity Over Reach Focus on replying, amplifying community voices, and celebrating others instead of chasing vanity metrics.
- Protective Guardrails Define topics, times, and lengths you'll engage—and stick to them.

Four Techniques to Weave Soul and Boundaries

1. Values Grid Planning

- Map your top four values to weekly content slots
- Rotate through them so every post feels aligned and authentic

1. "Quiet Day" Blocks

- Schedule 1–2 days weekly with zero posting or notifications
- Use that headspace for deep work, rest, or inspiration gathering

1. Response Templates with Personal Flare

- Draft short, warm reply frameworks ("Thank you for sharing that!")
- Customize one or two details before posting to save energy

1. Privacy Filters on Stories and Threads

- Curate what stays public versus what goes to close-friends lists or private groups
- Blur or redact sensitive details while keeping the core insight visible

Example Soulful Post Blueprint

SECTIONWHAT TO INCLUDE

Hook

A values-driven question or bold statement ("What if rest is your most radical act?")

Story Snippet

A 1–2 sentence anecdote tying back to your value grid

Insight

A clear takeaway or mini-framework ("Try the 3-step rest audit:...")

Boundary Note

A note on your engagement policy ("I'll be offline tomorrow but back in DMs Monday.")

Invitation

A question or prompt that honors reciprocity ("How do you guard rest in your week?")

Exercise: Design Your First Soulful Social Calendar

1. List your four core values for social outreach.
2. Assign each value to a day of the week.
3. Block at least one "quiet day" in your calendar.
4. Write one response template per value.
5. Draft three post hooks using the blueprint above.

Key Takeaways

- Grounding posts in values invites authentic engagement.
- Scheduled downtime days prevent burnout and spur fresh ideas.
- Simple templates save mental energy for real connection.
- Clear filters keep your private life private while sharing meaningful insight.

When to retreat, reset, and re-emerge

When to Retreat, Reset, and Re-emerge

DIRECT ANSWER: RECOGNIZE the signals you're drained, carve out deliberate pause periods, and design a clear re-entry plan so you return refreshed, focused, and aligned with your values.

Why Intentional Retreats Matter

TAKING STRATEGIC BREAKS isn't slacking—it's sharpening your edge.

- Prevents burnout before it derails your creativity
- Offers fresh perspective on stagnant projects
- Signals to your audience that self-care is part of your brand ethos

Three Signals It's Time to Step Back

1. Creative Drought

- Ideas feel forced or repetitive
- You catch yourself scrolling with no purpose

1. Emotional Overload

- Comments or DMs trigger anxiety instead of energy
- You react defensively or feel extra sensitive

1. Physical & Mental Fatigue

- Tension headaches, restless nights, or constant low mood
- Diminished focus on high-value tasks

Crafting Your Retreat & Reset Plan

PHASEFOCUSACTIONS

Prep
Set boundaries and inform community
Schedule "offline" notice; delegate or pause notifications
Retreat
Fully disconnect
Silence socials; color-coded do-not-disturb calendar blocks
Reset
Replenish mind, body, and spirit
Guided journaling; short nature walks; gentle movement practice
Re-emergence
Reconnect with purpose and audience
Share a "what I learned" post; update templates; relaunch goals

Five Steps to Re-emergence

1. Reflect on your retreat journal: note three insights or breakthroughs.
2. Edit your upcoming content calendar to align with fresh ideas.
3. Craft a comeback message that weaves in lessons and a values hook.
4. Re-enable notifications in staged intervals—start with comments only.
5. Schedule a brief debrief call or post to solidify accountability.

Exercise: Your Personal Retreat Blueprint

1. Identify your top two burnout signals from section 5.6.2.
2. Choose a retreat window (half-day, full-day, or multi-day).
3. List three restorative activities (e.g., forest walk, art therapy,

digital detox).

4. Sketch a simple re-emergence announcement using the table in 5.6.3.
5. Share your plan with a trusted peer or group for support.

Key Takeaways

- Scheduled retreats are as critical as content calendars.
- Clear boundary setting makes breaks guilt-free.
- A structured reset nourishes creativity and well-being.
- Thoughtful re-emergence rebuilds momentum and deepens trust.

7. Legacy Over Likes

Designing a brand that outlives trends

Designing a Brand That Outlives Trends

DIRECT ANSWER: ANCHOR your brand in enduring values, a flexible narrative, and an adaptable identity system—so you stay relevant when the next big thing arrives without chasing every fleeting fad.

Why Timeless Branding Matters

BUILDING A BRAND FOR the long haul means you:

- Cultivate trust instead of hype
- Save time and resources by avoiding constant overhauls
- Create emotional resonance that spans generations

When your foundation holds steady, you can bend with trends instead of breaking under them.

Four Pillars of Enduring Brands

- Core Values Define the unshakable principles guiding every choice, from messaging to partnerships.
- Narrative Flexibility Craft a brand story that accommodates new channels, audiences, and cultural shifts.
- Visual Timelessness Develop an identity system with signature elements and modular touches that evolve subtly.
- Audience-Centric Evolution Listen for changing needs and co-create your brand's next chapters with loyal fans.

Four Techniques to Future-Proof Your Brand

1. Archetypal Storytelling

- Anchor your narrative in classic archetypes (the Creator, Caregiver, Explorer)
- Swap in contemporary details while the core character remains constant

1. Adaptive Identity System

- Build a logo and color palette with primary and secondary tiers
- Create modular assets (icons, patterns, photo filters) you can refresh seasonally

1. Annual Brand Audit

- Review your visuals, voice, and values against emerging trends
- Retire or tweak only what no longer aligns, keeping the rest intact

1. Community-Led Innovation

- Run micro-focus groups or polls on potential pivots
- Empower brand ambassadors to pilot new ideas before full launch

Example Timeless Brand Blueprint

PILLARCORE COMPONENTFLEX Element

Core Values

Integrity, Empathy, Curiosity

Quarterly spotlight on impact story

Narrative
"The Journey of Creative Discovery"
New chapter theme each year
Visual Identity
Primary logo, serif typeface, signature green
Seasonal illustration set
Audience Evolution
Monthly feedback deep dive
Beta test private offering

Exercise: Chart Your Brand's Long Game

1. List your three non-negotiable values.
2. Write a one-sentence origin story using an archetype.
3. Audit your current logo, palette, and typography—tag what feels dated.
4. Brainstorm two modular identity elements you could swap each quarter.
5. Draft a mini-survey to capture audience feedback on one possible refresh.

Key Takeaways

- Timeless brands rest on values, not trends.
- Flexible narratives let you innovate without losing your soul.
- Modular visuals keep you fresh while preserving recognition.
- Co-creation with your community guides safe, meaningful evolution.

How to build impact without constant interaction

Building Impact Without Constant Interaction

DIRECT ANSWER: CREATE self-guided touchpoints, evergreen resources, and community-powered engines so your audience grows and thrives even when you're offline.

Why Asynchronous Impact Matters

SUSTAINED INFLUENCE doesn't require you to be "always on."

Delivering value that unfolds on its own respects both your energy and your audience's time.

It turns fleeting interactions into lasting transformation—without you fielding every question in real time.

Four Pillars of Low-Touch Influence

- Clarity of Promise Define precisely what change someone can achieve on their own, step by step.
- Evergreen Foundations Build resources that stay relevant—frameworks, templates, mini-courses.
- Autonomous Pathways Map self-guided journeys so people know exactly where to start and what comes next.
- Amplification Networks Equip advocates and peers to share, teach, and support newcomers independently.

Four Techniques to Scale Your Presence Silently

1. Signature Evergreen Content

- Record core lessons as on-demand videos, modular guides, or

interactive PDFs
- Update once a quarter, then let it work 24/7

1. Guided Automation Sequences

- Design an email or chat-bot series that delivers bite-size insights over weeks
- Embed reflection prompts and action tasks to sustain momentum

1. Community-Led Micro-Teams

- Invite experienced members to host small peer groups or accountability pods
- Provide them with discussion prompts and facilitator notes

1. Shareable Toolkits & Templates

- Package your frameworks into plug-and-play assets (spreadsheets, checklists, swipe files)
- Encourage users to remix and share their own versions—with credit back to you

Example Asynchronous Impact Blueprint

COMPONENTFORMATPURPOSE

Core Guide

PDF workbook + video walkthrough

Teach foundational framework without live teaching

Automated Email Sequence

7-day drip series

Reinforce lessons, invite reflection, and link tools

Peer-Group Starter Kit

Facilitator script + calendar

Scale small-group discussions without your presence
Share-Your-Win Channel
Branded hashtag + gallery page
Spotlight transformations, fuel social proof and reuse

Exercise: Build Your First Low-Touch Engine

1. Select one key transformation you deliver live.
2. Break it into a three-step guide or template.
3. Record a 5–7 minute walkthrough video.
4. Draft a short email sequence that unfolds one step per day.
5. Pilot with three loyal followers and gather feedback for tweaks.

Key Takeaways

- Impact that outlives you happens when learning paths are clear and self-sufficient.
- Automations amplify your voice while you recharge.
- Empowering community leaders multiplies your reach organically.
- Plug-and-play assets let advocates carry your teachings forward.

Turning your brand into a quiet revolution

Turning Your Brand into a Quiet Revolution

DIRECT ANSWER: SPARK meaningful change by embedding your core values into every interaction, rallying a devoted community around shared principles, and leveraging subtle, consistent actions that ripple outward without noise.

Why Quiet Revolution Works

BRANDS THAT WHISPER instead of shout build deeper loyalty.

Small, value-driven gestures compound over time, attracting like-minded supporters who become ambassadors for your mission.

This approach preserves your energy and authenticity while still shifting norms in your niche.

Four Pillars of a Quiet Revolution

- Purposeful Consistency Show up with the same guiding intention, aligning each touchpoint with your brand's "why."
- Community Empowerment Equip your audience to lead micro-initiatives under your brand's umbrella.
- Subversive Generosity Surprise and delight with unexpected resources, discounts, or VIP access for your most engaged allies.
- Ripple Messaging Craft messages designed for small circles—book clubs, private groups, peer pods—that then spread organically.

Four Techniques to Ignite Your Revolution

1. Values-Anchored Micro-Campaigns

- Launch a week-long challenge focused on one core value (e.g., "7 Days of Courageous Feedback")
- Share participant stories in a private gallery to fuel momentum

1. Ambassador Protocol Kits

- Provide ready-made graphics, swipe copy, and talking points for your top fans
- Encourage them to host local meetups or online salons

1. Hidden Easter Eggs

- Seed your content with subtle calls-to-action—secret hashtags, puzzle clues, or "golden tickets"
- Reward early decoders with exclusive content or collaborative opportunities

1. Whisper Network Channels

- Maintain a private forum or newsletter segment where your inner circle co-creates next moves
- Let them beta-test ideas before public rollout, weaving their feedback into final versions

Example Quiet Revolution Blueprint

COMPONENTACTIONOUTCOME

Micro-Campaign

"5 Days of Boundary Bravery" email series

100+ replies and user-generated tips shared
Ambassador Kit
Downloadable PDF with social postcards and conversation starters
15 community leaders hosting local salon nights
Easter Egg Hunt
Hidden link in blog posts leading to a private resource hub
30 highest-engaged users gain early access
Whisper Network
Monthly invite-only Zoom to co-design upcoming challenges
Co-hosted campaigns and 3x higher engagement rate

Exercise: Design Your Revolution Starter Kit

1. Define the single value you want to revolutionize (e.g., creative safety, radical honesty).
2. Sketch a micro-campaign around that value, including duration and core call-to-action.
3. List three assets your ambassadors will need (graphics, scripts, discussion prompts).
4. Choose one channel for your Whisper Network and draft an invitation message.
5. Outline a small reward system to recognize and amplify early participants.

Key Takeaways

- A quiet revolution leverages subtle, sustained actions over loud proclamations.
- Empowered ambassadors magnify your impact while honoring your boundaries.
- Unexpected acts of generosity foster deep goodwill and organic sharing.
- Private co-creation channels transform passive followers into

active collaborators.

⟐ Bonus Tools & Exercises

"Privacy Map" worksheet

Privacy Map Worksheet

DIRECT ANSWER: CHART your sharing zones, platform rules, and boundary guardrails so you lead with authenticity while protecting what matters most.

1. Clarify Your Privacy Zones

IDENTIFY THREE TIERS of sharing. Fill in each column to pinpoint what belongs where.

ZoneContent & DetailsWho Sees ItPlatform(s)Sharing Rules / Boundaries

Public

Community

Private

2. Pinpoint Sensitive Topics

USE THE PROMPTS BELOW to flag areas you'll treat as off-limits or semi-private.

1. I never share
2. I share only with close circles when...
3. I can talk about this publicly if I:

3. Platform-Specific Filters

DEFINE WHAT YOU'LL allow—or block—on each major channel.

PlatformAllowed ContentOff-Limits ContentEngagement Policy

Instagram

Twitter / X

LinkedIn

Newsletter

4. Establish Your Guardrail Prompts

WRITE AFFIRMATIONS or statements to anchor decisions in the moment.

- "Before posting, I ask: Does this serve my values and privacy zones?"
- "If sharing this detail feels uncomfortable, I pause and redact specifics."
- "My community guidelines prohibit X topic for my own well-being."

5. Maintenance & Review Schedule

SET REMINDERS TO REVISIT your map and adjust as needed.

CadenceAction
Weekly Check-In
Review next week's content against this map
Quarterly Audit
Update zones, topics, and platform filters based on new needs
Annual Retreat
Reflect on evolving boundaries and integrate fresh insights

"Persona Builder" template

Persona Builder Template

DIRECT ANSWER: CRAFT a rich, multi-dimensional profile of your ideal audience member—capturing their demographics, psychographics, goals, challenges, and media habits—so every message lands with precision and empathy.

1. Basic Profile

FIELDDETAILS

Persona Name
Age / Range
Occupation
Location
Photo or Icon
(Visual placeholder)

2. Demographics

- Age or age range
- Gender identity (if relevant)
- Education level
- Income bracket
- Family or household status

3. Psychographics

- Core values and beliefs
- Hobbies and interests
- Lifestyle and daily routines
- Personality traits (e.g., introverted, analytical, adventurous)

4. Goals & Motivations

- Primary goal (what they want most)
- Secondary goal (aspirations beyond primary)
- Long-term dreams or ambitions

5. Challenges & Pain Points

- Biggest professional or personal challenge
- Barriers preventing progress
- Emotional blockers or fears

6. Preferred Channels & Media Consumption

CHANNELFORMAT PREFERENCEFREQUENCY

Social media (specify)
Video / Carousel / Story
Daily / Weekly
Email newsletter
Short articles / Tips
Weekly / Monthly
Blog or website
Long-form articles
Monthly
Podcasts / Audio
Interviews / Solo shows
Bi-weekly

7. Brand Interaction Preferences

- Tone of voice (e.g., warm, direct, playful)
- Visual style (e.g., minimalist, vibrant, documentary)
- Level of formality and jargon
- Desired level of back-and-forth interaction

8. Customer Journey & Key Touchpoints

STAGEPERSONA ACTIONTOUCHPOINTCORE Need or Question

Awareness
Discovers content via search/ads
Blog post / Ad
"Is this relevant to me?"
Consideration
Reads case studies or testimonials
Email sequence
"Can this deliver results?"
Decision
Downloads a resource or signs up
Landing page
"Is it worth my time/money?"
Retention
Engages with community or content
Private group
"How do I keep progressing?"
Advocacy
Shares your work with peers
Social share
"Why should others know about this?"

9. Key Messaging Pillars

- Pillar 1: Core belief or promise to address primary goal
- Pillar 2: Empathy-driven proof that you understand their pain
- Pillar 3: Simple roadmap or framework for transformation
- Pillar 4: Invitation to engage or apply next steps

10. Empathy Map Prompts

- Says: What quotes or language would they use?
- Thinks: What worries or hopes occupy their mind?
- Does: What daily actions or behaviors reflect their needs?
- Feels: What emotions drive their decisions?

11. Next Steps & Validation

1. Create 2–3 distinct personas using this template.
2. Draft sample headlines, hooks, or emails tailored to each.
3. Test messaging with small focus groups or surveys.
4. Iterate based on feedback and observed engagement.

Boundary Scripts" for DMs, collabs, and interviews

Collection of Boundary Scripts for DMs, Collaborations, and Interviews

DIRECT ANSWER: USE these proven templates to express your limits with clarity and kindness in private messages, co-creation requests, and public conversations.

1. DM Boundaries

UNSOLICITED REQUESTS and personal curiosities thrive in DMs. Keep your peace with:

- **Availability Pause** "Hey [Name], thank you so much for the message. I'm taking a short break from DMs until [Date] to focus on [project/rest]. I'll get back to you then—thanks for your patience!"

- **Referral to Resources** "Hi [Name], I appreciate your question about [topic]. I've covered that in my [guide/blog post/link]. Let me know if that helps, and we can dive deeper after you've had a look."
- **Topic Off-Limits** "Thanks for asking about [topic]. I prefer to keep that part of my life private, but I'm happy to talk about [related topic] instead."

2. Collaboration Scripts

CO-CREATING CAN BLUR lines. Use these to define scope, time, and roles:

- **Scope Clarification** "Thank you for thinking of me for this project. To ensure it's a good fit, could we outline the key deliverables, deadlines, and decision-making process before proceeding?"
- **Decline With Appreciation** "I'm honored by the invitation to collaborate on [project]. My current focus is on [priority], so I'll have to pass this time. I'd love to explore possibilities in the future—let's stay in touch."
- **Feedback & Edit Boundaries** "I'm excited to contribute my section. For this piece, I'd like to limit revisions to two rounds and weigh in on any major shifts in direction to preserve the original intent."

3. Interview & Public Appearance Scripts

MAINTAIN CONTROL OVER your narrative during live or recorded conversations:

- **Time Commitment** "I can allocate [X] minutes for this interview. To make the most of our time, could we focus on [key themes]?"

- **Off-Limits Questions** "That's a thoughtful question, but I typically keep [personal detail] private. I'm happy to discuss [alternate topic] instead."
- **Topic Redirection** "Great point on [topic]. I'd also love to highlight [another relevant topic], as it ties back to our core discussion on [subject]."

4. Customization & Practice

1. Replace placeholders ([Name], [topic], [Date]) with your specifics.
2. Adjust the tone to match your brand—warmer, more succinct, or a bit more formal.
3. Rehearse aloud or role-play with a colleague to refine timing and delivery.

Key Takeaways

- Clear scripts protect your energy and reputation.
- Predefined templates reduce on-the-spot stress.
- Personalization keeps your brand authentic.
- Practice ensures you hold firm without hesitation.

"Visibility Audit" checklist

Visibility Audit Checklist

DIRECT ANSWER: SYSTEMATICALLY evaluate your presence, consistency, and impact across platforms to ensure your visibility aligns with your values, respects your boundaries, and serves your audience—without draining your energy.

1. Channel Presence & Profile Alignment

- List every platform where you maintain a profile (social, newsletter, podcast, blog).
- Verify each bio or about section reflects your core values and current offerings.
- Check that profile images, cover banners, and links are up to date.

2. Content Consistency & Cadence

- Review your posting schedule against your sustainable rhythm—are you hitting your intended frequency?
- Scan recent posts for consistent tone, voice, and visual style.
- Identify any gaps or "dark days" where you fell off your planned cadence.

3. Values & Messaging Alignment

- Pick five of your most recent posts and tag which core value each represents.
- Flag any content that feels off-brand or strays beyond your defined sharing zones.
- Ensure every piece of content delivers actionable

insight—even quick tips or reflections.

4. Privacy & Boundary Compliance

- Cross-reference your Privacy Map: were any off-limits topics accidentally shared?
- Confirm that DMs and comments adhered to your scripted responses and engagement policies.
- Note any boundary breaches and draft remediation steps (e.g., archive or redact).

5. Audience Engagement & Feedback

- Calculate your average response time to comments, DMs, and inquiries.
- Identify top three posts by engagement (likes, replies, shares) and analyze what resonated.
- Collect any unsolicited user feedback or survey responses about your visibility approach.

6. Technical Visibility Metrics

AUDIT AREACHECKPOINTSSTATUSNEXT Steps

SEO & Discoverability

Meta titles, descriptions, keywords, and backlink health

Email Deliverability

Open rates, click-throughs, bounce rates

Load Times & Accessibility

Page speed, mobile responsiveness, alt text, caption usage

Analytics Tracking

Goals, events, and funnels set up correctly in analytics tool

7. Accessibility & Inclusion

- Confirm all images have descriptive alt text.
- Check that videos include captions or transcripts.
- Review readability (font size, contrast) on your primary channels.

8. Action Planning & Review Cadence

1. Fill in status and notes for each table row above.
2. Identify the top three areas needing immediate attention.
3. Assign deadlines and owners (yourself or collaborators) for each action.
4. Schedule a monthly mini-audit to track progress.
5. Plan a quarterly deep dive to update your overarching visibility strategy.

Recap of "Build a Brand That Feels Like You"

This book equips privacy-conscious creators to anchor their brand in core values, set firm boundaries, and cultivate lasting impact—without burning out or oversharing.

1. Foundations: Values and Vision

YOU BEGIN BY DEFINING your non-negotiable principles and crafting a clear origin narrative. This ensures every choice—from messaging to partnerships—reflects your authentic "why."

Key takeaways

- Core values guide voice, visuals, and decisions
- A flexible brand story accommodates growth

2. Privacy and Boundaries

WITH THE PRIVACY MAP worksheet, you chart three sharing zones—public, community, private—and set platform-specific filters. Boundary scripts give you ready language for DMs, collabs, and interviews, so you protect your energy and reputation.

Key takeaways

- Tiered sharing zones prevent accidental oversharing
- Prewritten scripts ease hard "no" moments

3. Audience Intimacy Through Insight

RATHER THAN BEHIND-the-scenes access, you forge connection by revealing thought processes, anonymized case studies, and guided hypotheticals. Reflective prompts turn readers into collaborators, deepening trust without invasion.

Key takeaways

- Insight feels empowering; access can feel voyeuristic
- Structured blueprints ensure every post delivers value

4. Sustainable Presence

YOU LEARN TO BATCH themes, deploy modular templates, and align tasks with your peak energy windows. Accountability loops and recovery rituals transform showing up into a restorative rhythm, not a grind.

Key takeaways

- Sustainable cadences boost consistency and creativity
- Built-in rest protects against burnout

5. Social Media with Soul

POSTS ARE ROOTED IN your guiding values and tempered with protective guardrails. You balance intentional frequency with "quiet days," use response templates to save energy, and curate what stays public versus private.

Key takeaways

- Values-first content invites genuine engagement
- Scheduled downtime preserves mental clarity

6. Retreat, Reset, Re-emerge

RECOGNIZE CREATIVE droughts or emotional overload as signals to step back. Your retreat plan outlines prep, disconnection, restorative practices, and a staged re-entry—complete with a "what I learned" comeback message.

Key takeaways

- Intentional breaks sharpen your creative edge
- Structured re-emergence rebuilds momentum

7. Timeless Branding

YOU FUTURE-PROOF BY anchoring identity in archetypal storytelling, modular visual systems, and annual brand audits. Community-led innovation ensures you evolve in step with your audience, not fleeting fads.

Key takeaways

- Enduring brands rest on values, not trends
- Flexible frameworks let you adapt without losing soul

8. Asynchronous Impact

SIGNATURE EVERGREEN content, guided automation, peer micro-teams, and shareable toolkits let you influence quietly and powerfully. Your teachings live on while you recharge, and community leaders multiply your reach.

Key takeaways

- Clear self-guided pathways sustain impact
- Empowered advocates drive organic growth

9. Quiet Revolution

INSTEAD OF LOUD LAUNCHES, you spark micro-campaigns centered on one value, equip ambassadors with protocol kits, embed hidden "Easter eggs," and steward a private whisper network. Small, consistent actions ripple outward.

Key takeaways

- Subversive generosity fosters deep loyalty
- Ambassador-led initiatives amplify with minimal noise

Tools & Templates

THROUGHOUT THE BOOK you've filled out:

- Privacy Map
- Persona Builder
- Boundary Scripts swipe file
- Visibility Audit checklist

These plug-and-play assets keep your brand intentional, aligned, and resilient.

Also by Neil J Milliner

TheFreeMans Poetry Book
And So The Journey Begins
Artful Dwellings: Making Your House a Home With Beautiful Art
Artful Investments: Enhancing Your Property Value Through Fine Art
Art In The Workplace: Fostering Creativity and Innovation
E-commerce SEO Strategies: Selling Online Successfully
Delicious Vegetarian Pizzas For Everybody
I'm Married. Now What?: What To Do After "I Do!"
The Train Of Life
Fast Track Your Songwriting Career-Essential Tips and Hints to Master Your Craft and Build a Lasting Career
The Ultimate Singer's Guide
Branding & Networking Success for Bands
Mastering Fan Engagement-Pro-Level Hints to Create Authentic Connections and Build Loyalty
Mastering Live Performance & Touring-Pro Level Tips and Hints to Elevate Your Stage Presence and Tour Like a Pro
Music Production Mastery-Step-by-Step Tutorials to Fast-Track Your Way to Professional Success
The Musician's Marketing Playbook
The Musician's Tech Toolbox-Essential Technical Tips and Equipment Know-How for Musicians
The Ultimate Musician's Website Guide-Step-by-Step Tutorials to Engage Fans and Showcase Your Talent
How To Train Your Human: A Cat's Guide to Feline Mastery

The Bedroom Producers Blueprint
The Indie Artists Monetization Manual
Are You Going Out Like That?
The Time-Saving Myth: Why Efficiency Isn't Enough (And What Actually Works)
Building A Future From The Rubble Of The Past
How to Finish Creative Projects When You're Emotionally Fried
Manage Yourself Like a Boss
Build a Brand That Feels Like You
Master the Art of Saying No Without Guilt

Watch for more at https://neilmilliner.wixsite.com/motivated-informed.

www.ingramcontent.com/pod-product-compliance
Lightning Source LLC
LaVergne TN
LVHW090424210926
848480LV00002B/672